THE EXTRAORDINARY DADDY-LONG-LEGS RAILWAY OF BRIGHTON

Martin Easdown

AMBERLEY

As many of the illustrations in this book are taken from old postcards (the Edwardian era was the golden age of the postcard), it seems appropriate to feature a card issued in *c*. 1907 of the Pictorial Centre postcard shop at 18b Queens Road, Brighton, where cards of the Daddy-Long-Legs were probably available to purchase. The shop was opened by the German Rudolf Handwerck, who opened a second shop at 7 Grand Junction Road in 1907. He also published postcards in the Brighton Palace Series and other Handwerck cards can be seen in this book. The Queens Road shop closed in 1914, when Rudolf was forced to return to Germany due to the outbreak of the First World War.

Dedicated to the memory of Magnus Volk, a great Brightonian.

First published 2019

Amberley Publishing
The Hill, Stroud
Gloucestershire, GL5 4EP

www.amberley-books.com

British Library Cataloguing in Publication Data.
A catalogue record for this book is available from the British Library.

ISBN 978 1 4456 8935 7 (print)
ISBN 978 1 4456 8936 4 (ebook)

Typesetting by Aura Technology and Software Services, India.
Printed in Great Britain.

Contents

'The Spider Railway', as the Daddy-Long-Legs was sometimes known, heading towards the Paston Place terminus in December 1896. The flag displaying 'Brighton and Rottingdean' can clearly be seen.

A Wardell postcard from the 1920s showing the Daddy-Long-Legs and the Black Rock extension of the Volk's Electric Railway which replaced it. Magnus Volk's workshop and office can be seen in the lower view.

It Could Only Have Happened in Brighton

Thackeray, in *The Newcomers*, writes: 'It is the fashion to run down George IV, but myriads of Londoners ought to be thankful to him for inventing Brighton!' Although the town of Brighton, or 'Brighthelmstone', had existed and passed through eras of prosperity and depression, it was not until that monarch, then Prince of Wales in 1783, became attached to the place that it became a fashionable resort. Still, we may be thankful to the railway, opened in 1841, which from the frequency, cheapness and quickness of its trains enables such numbers of all classes of people to see this 'Queen of Watering Places' (*Seaside Watering Places 1897–8*, L. Upcott Gill).

An Edwardian advertising postcard issued by Brighton Corporation claiming that it has the grandest seafront in the world and the resort is available for health and pleasure the whole year round. An illustrated handbook was available on request. The view shows the West and Palace Piers.

The story of Brighton's ascent and development into a fashionable seaside watering place has been told many times. However, it's worth recapping that, in addition to George IV and the railway, its transformation from the humble fishing village of Brighthelmstone was also assisted by Dr Richard Russell's publication of *A Dissertation Concerning the Use of Seawater in Diseases of the Glands* in 1752, which advocated the drinking of, and bathing in, seawater to improve one's health. Dr Russell, from Lewes, built himself a residence in Brighton (now the site of the Royal Albion Hotel), and following his death in 1759 the house was rented to seasonal visitors. This included, in 1779, the brother of George III, the Duke of Cumberland. The Prince of Wales first came to Brighton on 7 September 1783 when he stayed with Cumberland, and liking the place, engaged Henry Holland in 1786 to design the Royal Pavilion, which was transformed by John Nash between 1815 and 1822 into a lavish oriental/Indian-influenced palace. Brighton experienced a peak period of growth between 1818 and 1828 when Charles Busby, Amon Wilds and Amon Henry Wilds built the Kemp Town Estate for Thomas Kemp in the east of the town and the Brunswick Town Estate at the other end, just across the Hove boundary.

Hotels such as the Royal York (1819), Royal Albion (1826) and Bedford (1829) were built for the increasing numbers of visitors, later joined by the sumptuous Grand (1864) and Metropole (1890). The first pleasure pier, the Chain Pier, was erected in

Picture postcards were sanctioned by the Post Office in 1894 on the proviso that the picture and message was on one side of the card and the address on the other. These early smaller size cards (known as court cards) were often attractively produced and some Brighton examples are shown in the following pages. This attractive card was published by W. Junor of Brighton in *c.* 1896 and features the Royal Pavilion, West Pier and the new Rottingdean Sea-going Car.

This is another postcard issued by W. Junor and shows Kings Road and the Metropole and Grand hotels. The card was sent to Germany on 28 April 1899.

1823 and its fame led to it being visited by three British monarchs and painted by Turner and Constable. It was joined by Eugenius Birch's West Pier in 1866; Birch also built the Aquarium in 1872. Pleasure gardens, baths, theatres and horse racing were also provided for the enjoyment of visitors, but towards the end of the Victorian era came the most extraordinary attraction of all: the Brighton and Rottingdean Seashore Electric Railway. Affectionately known as the 'Daddy-Long-Legs', but also termed the 'spider car', 'sea-going car', 'sea-going railway' and 'sea tramway', it presented the amazing spectacle of a part-tram, part-boat, part-seaside pier moving by itself through the sea like a seaborne cousin of one of the Martian fighting machines of H. G. Wells' *War of the Worlds*! Such was the novelty of the thing it was visited by the Prince of Wales in 1898.

Built by Magnus Volk as an extension of his Volk's Electric Railway, opened in 1883 and the oldest electric railway still running today, the Daddy-Long-Legs ran for only five years before new sea defence works forced its closure, and official abandonment in 1902. Volk was probably not too downhearted by its demise. Although very proud of his eccentric creation, it was unreliable, expensive to run and never profitable, and its demise led to Volk being able to extend his Volk's Electric Railway to Black Rock. Yet the Daddy-Long-Legs leaves a lasting impression on everyone who sees the old photographs of it and it rather typifies Brighton's Bohemian aspect. As my son Tom said: 'It could only have happened in Brighton.' Nearly 120 years after its demise, the Daddy-Long-Legs remains a Brighton icon, reproduced on postcards and posters, and it is a highlight of the new Volk's Railway Visitor Centre, where photographs, a trinket box and model of it are on display.

This court card, which has views of the West Pier, Aquarium and Hove Town Hall and was posted to Harrogate on 20 July 1902, was printed in Germany, as was the case with many coloured British picture postcards before the First World War.

The court cards were issued in the late 1890s during the time of the Daddy-Long-Legs and this card was sent on 20 July 1904 to Southampton and features views of the Royal Pavilion, St Peter's Church, Hotel Metropole and Volk's Electric Railway.

This court card was locally published by John E. Stafford of Brighton and Tunbridge Wells but was printed in Frankfurt-am-Main in Germany. It was posted to Paris on 12 August 1900 and features Eugenius Birch's two great Brighton creations – the West Pier (1866) and Aquarium (1872).

A court card with views of the Chain Pier, Queens Park and the nearby town of Lewes. The Chain Pier was destroyed by a storm in December 1896 but was still to feature on postcards for some time (as was the Daddy-Long-Legs). Queens Park was donated to the town in 1890 by the Race Stand Trustees and the illustration shows the drinking fountain which can still be seen there. The card was also sent to France, to Bourges, on 28 July 1902, but the publisher is not stated.

The Daddy-Long-Legs is one of the three illustrations on this court card. The card was sent to an address in Ipswich on 8 August 1904, by which time the sea-going railway had been closed for two years.

Views of the Metropole and Grand Hotels, Old Steine, Rottingdean Church and Devil's Dyke feature on this court card from the late 1890s.

This court card has managed to cram in five views of Brighton and one of Devil's Dyke. The Dyke is a popular beauty spot on the South Downs above Brighton and the illustration shows the aerial cableway that spanned the deep gorge between 1894 and 1909. The postcard, which was not used, was produced by J. F. Bigwood at the Swiss Warehouse, 71 Kings Road, Brighton, and was printed in Germany.

Another W. Junor court card, which features Kings Road, the Aquarium and Old Steine. The card was posted to Hampstead on 25 November 1899.

Although the Daddy-Long-Legs was unique, there was a similar looking machine that ran between the harbours of St Malo and St Servan in northern France, which perhaps inspired Magnus Volk to build his railway through the sea. Known as Le Pont Roulant (the rolling bridge or crane), it was the one and only cousin of the Daddy-Long-Legs, as charmingly described by Henri Fermin in his excellent publication in French *L'e Popee du Pont Roulant de Saint Malo a Saint Servan et de Son Seul et Unique Cousin le Daddy Long Legs de Brighton* (1999). Fermin's book details the history of Le Pont Roulant with lots of photographs and has a chapter on the Daddy-Long-Legs, so it seems only right to feature Le Pont Roulant in this publication.

The Daddy-Long-Legs has inevitably featured in many books on Brighton's past, but here, for the first time, it is the centrepiece. Hop aboard for a remarkable train ride through the sea.

The 'Sea Railway' features on this court card of Brighton issued by Valentines and posted to Liverpool on 29 October 1900.

A postcard produced for the Christmas market in the late 1890s featuring a rather unusual subject matter for the festive season: the destruction of the Chain Pier in December 1896.

Magnus Volk: A Great Innovator and Dreamer

The Great Brighton inventor and electrical engineer Magnus Volk was born at 35 (now 40) Western Road on 19 October 1851, the son of a German clockmaker. He married Anna Banfield in 1879 and they went on to have seven children. Volk inherited his father's engineering talents and installed the first telephone and electric light systems in Brighton at his home at 51 Preston Street. In 1881 he was awarded a gold medal for an innovative fire alarm system linked directly to the police station, and two years later Brighton Corporation asked him to install electricity in the Royal Pavilion. Volk also dabbled in building electric cars, including one for the Sultan of Turkey, but it was to be in the field of electric railways that he was to make his name.

The first electric tramway was demonstrated by Fyodor Pirotsky in St Petersburg in 1880, and in 1881 Werner von Siemens operated an electrically powered line in the Lichterfeld district of Berlin. That same year saw Siemens build a small demonstration electric railway in the grounds of the Crystal Palace in London. This was seen by Volk and it gave him the idea to build a similar line in Brighton. On 14 June 1883, he wrote to the Town Clerk of Brighton Corporation seeking permission to open a 2-foot gauge electric railway from the Aquarium to the Chain Pier, a length of 440 yards (402 metres). This was granted, and Volk wasted no time in building the line, which took

Magnus Volk (1851–1937), the mind behind the unique Daddy-Long-Legs, one of the most unusual railways to have been built in Britain.

only eighteen days to construct. On 4 August 1883 Volk opened the first public electric railway in Britain. It was powered by a 2 hp Crossley gas engine and Siemens D5 50 V DC dynamo (which formerly powered the electricity in Volk's house) placed in the Royal Humane Society's arch under the promenade. The 50 V output ran via cables to the running rails, which were laid by Messrs T. Chappell on the shingle ballast close to the sea wall on Madeira Road (now Madeira Drive), above the high-water mark. The single wooden passenger car, built by Messrs Pollard, could seat around ten passengers and was powered by a ½ hp electric motor receiving its current via the running wheels. The car could be driven at either end to a maximum speed of 6 mph.

In its first five months, Volk's Electric Railway carried over 30,000 passengers, and Volk was granted permission to extend the line east to the Paston Place Groyne, Kemp Town, after his plan to extend west to Hove was refused. Commonly referred to as the 'Banjo Groyne' on account of its shape, the groyne was built by Brighton Corporation of stone in 1877 and was a popular promenade known as the 'Free Pier'. Volk planned to connect the new terminus to Marine Parade above with a water-balance lift laid on the western flight of steps. Two cars, each seating five people, were to be provided, but as the lift was nearing completion in January 1884 at a cost of £500, it was dismantled due to the vociferous opposition of residents. The extension to the railway was opened

The opening day of the Volk's Electric Railway on 4 August 1883. The original single passenger car is at the Aquarium end of the line and Magnus is standing on the car platform on the left with Mayor Cox on the right platform. Mrs Volk is sitting inside the car on the left.

A cabinet photo shows the Aquarium station of Volk's Electric Railway soon after the line was extended to Paston Place, Kemp Town, in 1884. One of the two open-ended four-wheeled mahogany cars built that year can be seen. They could seat up to thirty passengers at a speed of 8 mph. The company's title above the station canopy is of interest as it includes the lift that was partially built on the Paston Place steps before it was abandoned. The Chain Pier is in the background.

on Friday 4 April 1884, bringing the length of the line to 1,400 yards (1,316 metres). A track gauge of 2 feet 8½ inches was adopted and the line passed under the Chain Pier by means of a timber-lined cutting. Two new double-ended four-wheel cars, powered by a 6 hp Siemens motor and with a capacity to carry around twenty-two passengers, were provided. A new 12 hp Crossley Otto gas engine provided the power to drive a Siemens D2 dynamo housed in the Paston Place Arch at the bottom of Duke's Mound, which was leased by Volk from Brighton Corporation. The first floor of the arch was used initially as a waiting room before becoming an office, while the ground floor became the maintenance workshop, accessed by a line laid across Madeira Road.

The newly extended line proved to be very popular, but continual damage by stormy seas led to the track being raised above sea level on a timber viaduct in 1886. At the same time, a third rail for electric pick-up was installed to reduce leakages caused by seawater. The cost of these improvements, however, led to Magnus Volk filing for bankruptcy in January 1888. The railway was kept running, and upon Volk's discharge from bankruptcy in October 1891, the grand dreamer was keen to realise his vision for an extension of his railway to Rottingdean.

The Aquarium station as seen from the Palace Pier in 1910 with two cars in the platforms. Note the sign, which states that the return fare along the line was 4*d*, and the shop under the station.

A postcard in the A&G Taylor's Reality Series showing the Volk's Electric Railway Aquarium station looking west in *c*. 1910. The car on the right is loaded and will soon be ready to depart. The tall 'Electric Railway' sign is prominently displayed for all to see.

S 5299   ELECTRIC RAILWAY BRIGHTON.

This view, published in the WHS 'Kingsway' Series and sent on 17 March 1914, was taken on the platform and shows a car arriving at the station viewed by onlookers on the promenade. A flag on the beach shows that the bathing machines are open for business.

A postcard produced by Pictorial Centre at 7 Grand Junction Road, Brighton (using a Valentines photograph), showing a view of Volk's Electric Railway taken from the Chain Pier, which must date it before late 1896. The car is heading east towards the pier.

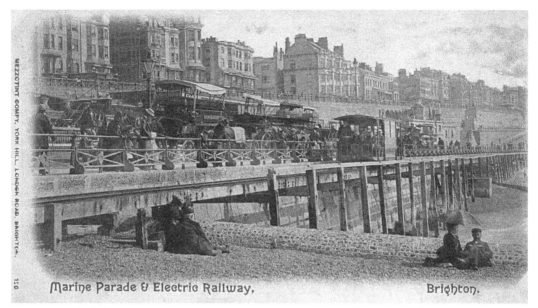

This postcard published by Mezzotint was sent to Jersey on 30 March 1905 and shows the Volk's Electric Railway car heading towards Aquarium station. A line of horse brakes can be seen lining the road, and in the background can be seen the Old Chain Pier Bazaar with a camera obscura on the roof. On the cliff top, Marine Parade was laid out between 1830 and 1838.

Posted on 30 September 1912, this postcard of Volk's Electric Railway shows the car travelling towards Paston Place. Prominent are the arches of Madeira Terrace, constructed in 1890, which are Grade II listed but at the time of writing need restoring. In the background is the Madeira Lift, which was opened on 24 May 1890.

A view further east along Madeira Road showing the Volk's Electric Railway car heading west to the Aquarium. The card was published by Sidney Hellier and was posted to Blankenberghe, Belgium, on 13 August 1904.

The original terminus of Volk's Electric Railway was at the Chain Pier before the line was extended to Paston Place in 1884. This postcard, published by Sidney Hellier and posted on 13 February 1903 (over six years after the pier's demise in December 1896), shows the Volk's car near the cutting under the pier. The card has been attractively hand-coloured.

A photograph of the Volk's Electric Railway car about to enter the Chain Pier cutting from the eastern side. The Chain Pier's attractive entrance kiosks can still be found today on the Palace Pier. The suspension chains of the pier can be seen going into H. Snelling's Royal Chain Pier Bazaar, which was demolished in the 1920s.

The Volk's Electric Railway car can just be seen by the cutting under the Chain Pier in the early 1890s in this postcard of Marine Parade, published some ten years later by Sidney Hellier and sent on 16 September 1903. The chief interest of the view is that it shows the short period (between 1891 and 1896) when Brighton had three piers, although the Palace Pier in the centre is still under construction.

A postcard of the Paston Place station and car shed of Volk's Electric Railway adjoining the Banjo Groyne. The card was posted on 13 March 1905 by Edward to Miss Talbot at Henley-on-Thames and he tells her that 'these cars run close to the edge of the sea'.

Triumph: The Daddy-Long-Legs Is Unveiled to a Curious Public

The original plan to carry the railway on a viaduct for the 2-mile 1,628-yard extension to Rottingdean was quickly deemed too expensive and Volk conceived the remarkable plan to build the line through the sea and have the passenger car placed on legs to clear the high-water mark. Financial backing was received from Edmund Overall Bleackley of Kemp Town, who became chairman of the newly formed Brighton & Rottingdean Seashore Electric Tramroad Company (although the completed line was built as a railway and become known as such). The company had a capital of £20,000 and powers to borrow a further £5,000. Engineer Richard St George Moore, designer of the Palace Pier under construction just to the west of the Volk's Electric Railway Aquarium station, was engaged to design the passenger car and the jetties needed to receive it. His plans were received by the Board of Trade on 30 November 1892, and having been approved, the Act of Parliament for the extension of the Volk's Electric Railway from Paston Place, Kemp Town, to Rottingdean Gap, to be completed within three years, was granted on 27 July 1893 without any opposition. Construction commenced in June 1894; however, progress was slow as the work had to be carried out at low tide. The pier at Rottingdean was completed first and it was opened to the public on occasions from 11 June 1895. The seashore railway's generator of electricity was located beneath the pier and consisted of a 100 hp steam engine (provided by Sissons & Co. of Gloucester) driving a 60 kW dynamo. This gave a traction voltage of 500 V, which generated electricity to an overhead cable supported by wooden poles placed along the length of the line. The cable would be in contact with the wheels of the twin trolley poles (originally one pole was provided but a second was quickly added for safety) of the passenger car for continual positive and return current. This would pass through the four 24-foot-high pier-like legs of the car to the bogies at the bottom of each leg, which each housed four 33-inch wheels. One bogie on each side of the car was driven by a shaft and worm-gear arrangement from two 25 hp electric motors, while the other two housed the brake rodding. The return current then passed through the rails, and the sea at high tide. The passenger car had tram-like controllers at each end of the main deck and was to run upon two parallel lines of rails laid 18 feet apart, which formed a single railway of 2 feet 8½ gauge. The flat-bottomed rails were laid upon 5 x 3-foot concrete slabs placed 60–100 yards away from the cliff. Gradients of 1 in 100 were placed at both termini to assist in starting and stopping the car.

Richard St George Moore (1858–1926) designed the car and landing stages for the Brighton & Rottingdean Seashore Electric Railway. Moore was a civil engineer of some distinction and a pier specialist. He was responsible for the design of both St Leonards Pier (opened 1891) and Brighton's Palace Pier (opened 1899) and this probably influenced Magnus Volk to engage him for his sea-going railway project. *Pioneer* certainly had the appearance of a section of pier moving through the sea by itself!

Richard St George Moore's Brighton Palace Pier, photographed in 1906. Moore was also responsible, among other works, for an extension to Ryde Pier, the Paris Big Wheel, West Hampshire Waterworks and the Marlborough & Grafton Railway. His practice was situated at 17 Victoria Street, Westminster, London.

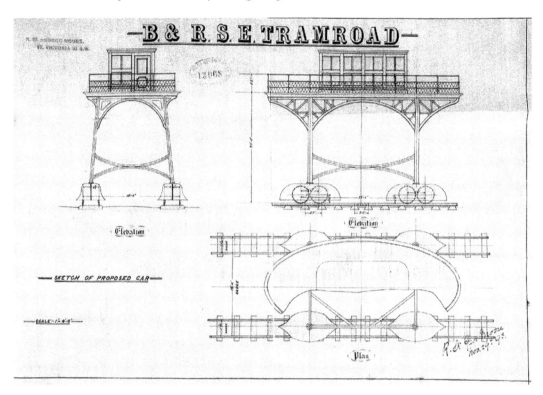

Richard St George Moore's original design for the car of the Brighton & Rottingdean Seashore Electric Railway, dated 29 November 1893. The cross-bracing between the legs was to change, and the car is missing the upper deck on the saloon and the safety features such as the lifeboat and lifebuoys.

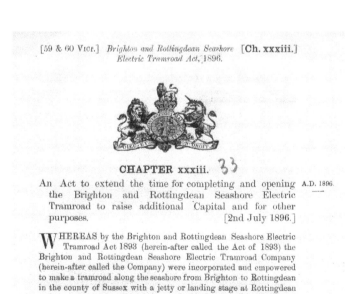

[59 & 60 VICT.] *Brighton and Rottingdean Seashore* [**Ch. xxxiii.**]
Electric Tramroad Act, 1896.

CHAPTER xxxiii. *33*

An Act to extend the time for completing and opening   A.D. 1896.
the Brighton and Rottingdean Seashore Electric
Tramroad to raise additional Capital and for other
purposes.   [2nd July 1896.]

WHEREAS by the Brighton and Rottingdean Seashore Electric
    Tramroad Act 1893 (herein-after called the Act of 1893) the
Brighton and Rottingdean Seashore Electric Tramroad Company
(herein-after called the Company) were incorporated and empowered
to make a tramroad along the seashore from Brighton to Rottingdean
in the county of Sussex with a jetty or landing stage at Rottingdean
and to raise twenty thousand pounds by shares and five thousand
pounds by borrowing :

The Act of Parliament, passed on 2 July 1896, allowing an extension of time for completing the Brighton & Rottingdean Seashore Electric Tramroad.

The splendid passenger car, which was a curious hybrid of a pier, yacht and tram, was constructed by the Gloucester Railway Carriage & Wagon Company. The main deck consisted of a 45 x 22-foot elliptical platform with a saloon in its centre measuring 25 x 12 feet. The inside of the saloon was decorated in light brown and white and fitted with a fine upholstered ottoman down its centre, stained glass windows, plush curtains and carpets, potted plants and a refreshment booth. A ladder on the outside of the saloon led to an open upper deck, which had a central seating area and further seats lining the railing. There was also seating on the main platform. The car weighed 45 tons and was licensed to carry 150 passengers. Volk named it *Pioneer*, perhaps in honour of himself!

The Brighton terminus of the seashore railway consisted of a light steel jetty situated just to the east of the Banjo Groyne and a short walk from the terminus of the Volk's Electric Railway. The jetty housed waiting rooms and offices and was constructed by the local firm of Charles German Reed & Son of North Street.

With the three-year period of the Brighton & Rottingdean Seashore Electric Tramroad Act 1893 having ran out, a new act for completing the line by July 1898 was granted on 2 July 1896. The act also gave the company power to raise any additional capital not exceeding £8,000 by the issue of new ordinary and preference shares of no less than £10 in value. The line was completed in time for a Board of Trade inspection on 12 September 1896, which saw the car worked at both high and low tides. However, the inspector noticed several faults which needed to be rectified before an operating certificate could be issued. The flaws included an incomplete sleeper formation and the absence of securing nails, cast iron sleeper chains and a buffer stop at Rottingdean. Regarding the car, fire

Pioneer as newly built by the Gloucester Railway Carriage & Wagon Company. Clearly seen are the side doors of the saloon, the staircase to the upper deck and the central seating on the upper deck. The safety features, additional seating and trolley poles have yet to be added.

A further view of *Pioneer* as originally built by the Gloucester Railway Carriage & Wagon Company. The car must surely have been the most unusual vehicle the company ever built.

buckets and railings around the driver at each end needed to be added, and enhancing the maritime flavour of the venture, a ship's bell, flag, lifebuoys and a lifeboat with companion ladder were to be put in place. The staff were to wear naval-type uniforms, and because it was a sea-going vessel, the driver had to be a qualified 'ship's captain' familiar with the coast and able to ascertain weather and sea conditions. Furthermore, there was to be a speed limit of 8 mph, no running in bad weather and a daily inspection of the track. A telephone system was put in place in case of emergencies. A second inspection found the necessary alterations and additions had been carried out and an operating licence was issued. The total cost of the venture was £30,000.

The ceremonial opening was fixed for noon on Saturday 28 November 1896 and present on the day at the Brighton terminus were the Mayor of Brighton, Alderman Blaker, and the Chairman of Rottingdean Parish Council, Mr Steyning Beard, who were accompanied by members of Brighton Town Council and other invited guests. Following a quick out and in journey for the Mayor, who had another function to attend, *Pioneer* set out for the 35-minute journey to Rottingdean. The *Brighton and Hove Guardian* on 2 December 1896 reported that on the opening day:

> … Large crowds of people assembled to view the spectacle, especially on the Paston Place Groyne from which the car appeared to be one dense mass of people. The day was a beautiful one, hardly a cloud seen in the sky, but a biting north-east wind caused those in the car to stamp about a good deal in the vain attempt of getting a little warm. The ceremony was timed to take place at twelve o'clock, but it was half-an-hour later before a start was made. During the wait, appropriated souvenirs of the railway were distributed to the company and were heartily appreciated. In the souvenir were photographs of the car at high tide, in a storm and at low tide; and another of the interior of the car.
>
> At half-past twelve, the Mayor, accompanied by the Mayoress, set the car going amid cheering from the onlookers. After about fifty yards had been traversed the machinery was reversed and

25

we were speeding back to our destination. Speculation was rife as to the cause of this. Rumour said that it was only intended to go as far as the new groyne (at Black Rock) because of the cold east wind, but those present had not really commenced to feel the cold yet. At five-and-twenty minutes to one, the serious start was made, and the easy gliding motion of the car soon became apparent to all. Now and again there was a little oscillation, but that was due, we were informed, to the sand that collected on the rails. Owing to it being low tide, those present were enabled to inspect the rails and concrete blocks and noticed for themselves the stability of the work. The journey, which is six miles there and back, took 32 minutes in going and 36 in returning and proved a delightful one. As we neared the Rottingdean Pier, two young ladies waved their hands in response to the lusty cheers of the assembled onboard. Some of the inhabitants, not so bold, watched the approach of the car from a distance, as though they did not care to be introduced too abruptly to the amphibious creature. The return journey proved far pleasant than the outward one, as, this time, the car was travelling with the wind instead of against it.

Having arrived at Paston Place Groyne, the company rapidly gathered in the Madeira Road Hall where a luncheon was served.

A photograph published in the *Illustrated London News* of 5 December 1896 showing *Pioneer* at the Paston Place Jetty on 28 November 1896, ready to depart on its inaugural journey. The jetty is bedecked with flags and large crowds are gathered on the beach, Banjo Groyne and Marine Parade. They had never seen anything remotely like this before.

Right: The Mayor of Brighton, Alderman Blaker, starts the controls of *Pioneer* for its first trip on the opening day of 28 November 1896. The Mayor only enjoyed a short journey as he had another engagement to attend.

Below left: *Pioneer* is seen at the Paston Place Jetty ready for boarding on its inaugural run on 28 November 1896.

Below right: *Pioneer* setting off on its first journey with the dignitaries aboard on 28 November 1896.

A postcard issued in *c.* 1910 by Thomas Wiles of Hove showing *Pioneer* without its lifeboat and lifebuoys at the Paston Place Jetty in 1896. The junction of Paston Place with Marine Parade can be seen upper left.

Local photographer A. W. Wardell published this postcard in *c.* 1920 of *Pioneer* at the Paston Place Jetty in 1896, proving that, even twenty years after closure, there was still an interest in this most remarkable of railways. This photograph and the previous one are of the same journey (note the men sitting on the jetty in both views) but Wardell has retouched his by adding the lifeboat and lifebuoys and redrawing the properties on Marine Parade.

A view of the plush interior of *Pioneer* with its central ottoman, potted plants, carpet and curtains. Magnus Volk can be seen sitting on the ottoman.

A further view of the interior of *Pioneer*. Note the pretty flowered light on the ceiling.

The public service was commenced on Monday 30 November 1896 with the headline 'A Sea Voyage on Wheels'. The fare was *6d* each way (*3d* for children). Unsurprisingly, this new and unique railway was inundated with customers, who waited patiently on the Brighton terminus jetty for their turn to experience a ride through the sea. A bright future seemingly awaited this most unusual of railways, but before the week was out the Daddy-Long-Legs was to endure a night of unprecedented havoc.

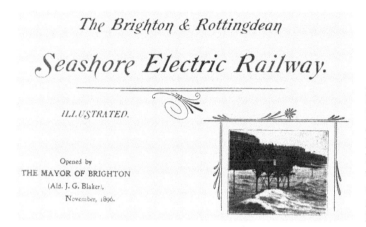

The Brighton & Rottingdean

Seashore Electric Railway.

ILLUSTRATED.

Opened by
THE MAYOR OF BRIGHTON
(Ald. J. G. Blaker),
November, 1896.

An eight-page illustrated brochure was issued by Magnus Volk to celebrate the opening of his sea-going railway in November 1896. These were available to purchase aboard the car, but not many examples appear to have survived.

A Brief Description of

The Brighton & Rottingdean Seashore Electric Railway.

THE idea of this unique Railway originated with Mr. MAGNUS VOLK, of the Electric Railway, Brighton, but it would never have been brought to a successful completion in the face of so many difficulties had it not been for the untiring efforts and the very substantial financial support of the other Directors, Messrs. E. O. BLEACKLEY, J. J. CLARK, and R. J. POPE.

Mr. ST. GEORGE MOORE, M.I.C.E., of Westminster, acted as Co-Engineer with Mr. VOLK.

Parliamentary Powers were obtained in June, 1893, and the total Capital of the Company is £35,000.

The Railway runs through the sea between Brighton and Rottingdean, three miles away, on rails laid on concrete blocks, spaced about three feet apart, and morticed into the sound rock; the height of the blocks varying with the irregularities of the shore. The steepest gradient is 1 in 300, and the radius of curves 40 chains.

The line consists of double parallel tracks, each being 2 feet 8½ inches gauge; thus giving an effective gauge of 18 feet, this being necessary to give the required stability to the Cars.

In addition to containing photographs, the brochure gave a brief description of the railway, including technical details.

A photograph from Volk's brochure showing *Pioneer* at the Paston Place Jetty at low tide during pre-opening testing.

This view in the brochure of *Pioneer* in a storm was a foretaste of what was soon to come during the night of 4–5 December 1896.

The famous poster of the Daddy-Long-Legs, reproduced many times since, advertising 'A sea voyage on wheels' for a fare of *6d* each way.

Disaster: A Night of Unprecedented Havoc

Magnus Volk was warned that a severe storm was to hit the Brighton area during the night of 4–5 December 1896 and in anticipation of this he lashed *Pioneer* to the end of Rottingdean Pier. When the storm duly arrived, it was to cause widespread damage in Brighton, including to Volk's new sea-going railway. The old condemned Chain Pier, closed the previous October after being declared unsafe, was washed away save for the first tower, and the entrance kiosks and its great timbers repeatedly smashed against the piles of the Paston Place Jetty until it was left 'all but an utter wreck. Many of the piles were broken away, the roof was broken and twisted, and the floors smashed' (*Southern Weekly News*, 12 December 1896). The timbers of the Chain Pier also broke through the shore end piling of the West Pier, causing extensive damage, and collided with the unfinished Palace Pier. Volk's pride and joy, *Pioneer*, was wrecked after breaking free from its moorings at Rottingdean Pier, which suffered structural damage. The *Southern Weekly News* of 12 December 1896 gave a vivid description of the damage caused to the railway: 'Here for all one knows, it may have made a bold stand against wind and waves for some time, but the pressure on the shoreward set of rails proved too great for the stability of the line. Daylight and low tide revealed three or four blocks of concrete overturned, a rail bent in a V-shape, and, near to this spot, the car reduced to a shapeless ruin. The huge iron feet, those sheaths in which the cog-wheel machinery worked, were lying overturned on the sand. The lower deck lay almost flat on the beach, the brass rails for a large part broken; but shreds of velvet still clung about the ruins with a sort of pathetic fidelity.'

The storm-damaged Paston Place Jetty seen from the promenade on the morning of 5 December 1896.

The shattered Paston Place Jetty following the storm of 4–5 December 1896, clearly showing the extent of the damage to the building housing the waiting room and office. The supporting piling was also twisted, which necessitated the demolition of the structure.

Another view of the wrecked Paston Place Jetty following the storm of 4–5 December 1896.

The severely damaged Paston Place Jetty was quickly demolished, leaving twisted metalwork for local children to climb on. This in turn was soon removed, leaving little trace that the jetty ever stood there.

A photograph of Rottingdean Pier after the storm of 4–5 December 1896 that was reproduced in the *Brighton Visitor* on 9 December 1896. The pier remained standing but has lost most of its decking. There is also no sign of the electricity generator underneath the pier head that can be seen in most photographs of the pier.

The Chain Pier, which had been closed two months previously as it was unsafe, was largely demolished by the storm of 4–5 December 1896, save for the entrance kiosks and the first tower. That was the end for this famous old Brighton landmark and its successor, the Palace Pier, can be seen under construction in the background. Volk's Electric Railway was also extensively damaged and in the photograph above young boys can be seen climbing on its twisted track.

The shore end of the West Pier was extensively damaged by wrecked timbers from the dying Chain Pier during the night of 4–5 December 1896.

Fleeting Halcyon Days:
Pioneer at Banjo Groyne

Undeterred, Volk was determined to rebuild his sea-going railway. *Pioneer* was salvaged by Messrs Blackmore, Gould & Company of Millwall and was restored with its legs 2 feet taller than before. The remains of the wrecked Paston Place Jetty were removed, and a simpler landing stage was built out from the eastern side of the Banjo Groyne to give a wider frontage to the passenger car. On 20 July 1897, the railway was reopened without great ceremony and for the rest of the year 44,282 passengers were carried.

Pioneer is seen approaching the replacement landing stage on the Banjo Groyne following the reopening of the railway on 20 July 1897. The jetty has no covered waiting area like its predecessor, just a small ticket hut for staff. The car is loaded to capacity.

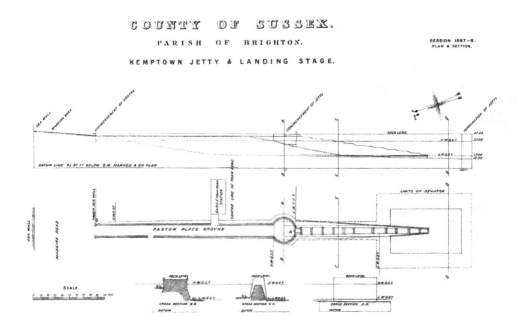

Richard St George Moore's proposal in November 1897 for a Kemp Town jetty and landing stage to be placed on the end of the Banjo Groyne; nothing came of the scheme.

In November 1897, Richard St George Moore presented the Board of Trade with a proposal to extend the Banjo Groyne by 250 feet to 600 feet to provide a new 'Kemp Town Jetty and Landing Stage'. However, the scheme was soon abandoned.

The railway received a royal visitor on 20 February 1898 when the Prince of Wales took two trips on it: one in the morning and an afternoon ride in the company of Magnus Volk, who placed a commemorative plaque in the saloon of *Pioneer*. An hourly service to Rottingdean was announced for the summer of 1898, but this soon proved impossible to keep to. This was due to a return journey along the full length of the line taking up to 2 hours at an average speed of 6 mph. At high tide, the underpowered car would crawl at a walking pace and the journey could become quite tedious. A single car was inadequate to provide a regular service and return journeys became limited to three per day. *Pioneer* was often fully loaded and large numbers of potential passengers were left behind, leading to long queues on Banjo Groyne. Mechanical problems with *Pioneer* and bad weather could bring the service to a halt. A second passenger car, and more powerful motors for *Pioneer*, were both proposed to speed up the service, but lack of finance due to heavy construction and maintenance costs meant these never materialised.

However, there was no denying that a journey on *Pioneer* was a unique and unusual experience, especially when it was ploughing through a high tide of 15 feet of water. The *Morning Post* commented that it was 'a railway which carried its passengers over the surface of the sea to afford all the pleasurable sensation of a yachting trip without fear of "Mal de Mer" is a thing so strange and unlike every engineering enterprise yet conceived that it merits more than a passing notice'.

Pioneer approaching the Banjo Groyne Jetty in the late 1890s, with the car appearing to be lightly loaded. The photo was later utilised as a postcard sent on 26 August 1911.

This view shows *Pioneer* more heavily loaded, particularly on the upper deck. Judging by all the parasols on display, it must have been a hot day.

On 28 February 1899 a meeting of the Brighton & Rottingdean Seashore Electric Tramroad Company took place where it was sadly reported that the founder and chairman of the company, Mr E. O. Bleackley, had passed away. It was stated that *Pioneer* ran throughout 1898 except during spells of stormy weather, which fortunately had caused no damage to either the car or the track. The number of passengers carried was 112,548, earning total receipts of £2,752 3s 3d. Of this sum, £1,616 19s 3d was earned during the months June to September and it was felt that this could have been doubled if there had been a second car. Overall, receipts were good, but not equal to what had been anticipated. The autumn had been a very wet and stormy one and receipts had been several hundred pounds less than anticipated.

On a more positive note, with the electric supply now being obtained from Brighton Corporation, staff numbers could be reduced, leading to a reduction in working expenses of around £300–400 for next year. The car would also have a little more power, leading to more trips being made. The working expenditure for 1898 had been about 60 per cent of the takings, which was a large proportion out of a gross profit of £892 17s 2d. The sum of £105 had to be paid to Lloyds for insurance of the car and jetties, and there were other standing expenses which reduced the profit available for interest and the dividends to around £500, or, if the company had no debentures or losses, enough to pay 1½ per cent on the capital of the company. Negotiations had been taking place with a firm to build a second car and paying for it in instalments over three or four years as the company's capital was exhausted. However, as noted earlier, the second car was never built.

BRIGHTON.

We are now going to look at some of the postcards that were issued of the Daddy-Long-Legs during its short lifespan and in the immediate years after. This court size card is by an unknown publisher. A sign on the jetty can be seen stating 'Rottingdean and Back'.

This card, by the same unknown publisher as the previous view, was sent to an address in Hove on 17 July 1898 with the message 'I have seen the above electrical novelty which runs through the sea to Rottingdean!'

A court size card of the sea-going car (as it was often termed) with a message in French and posted to Boulogne on 22 October 1899. A sizeable proportion of the cards showing the Daddy-Long-Legs were sent to the Continent, with both the sender and receiver no doubt intrigued by what they saw.

Above: I wonder what Mr Wolff of Halle in Germany thought of the sea-going car when he received this postcard on 30 December 1899?

Left: *Pioneer* is seen docked at the Banjo Groyne Jetty on this colourful court size postcard sent to Vienna on 19 March 1900.

Right: The timetable for the 'Brighton Electric Sea Railway' for the service week ending 1 October 1899, which proudly proclaims it was patronised by HRH the Prince of Wales (he enjoyed two rides on it on 20 February 1898).

Below: The other side of the timetable leaflet showing the journey times. Short trips out from Banjo Groyne were also available in addition to the full journey along the line to Rottingdean.

A COOL AND PLEASANT SEA VOYAGE ON WHEELS.

BRIGHTON & ROTTINGDEAN ELECTRIC SEA RAILWAY TIME TABLE SEE OTHER SIDE

Patronised by H.R.H.

The PRINCE OF WALES.

THE SEA-GOING CAR *(Licensed by the Board of Trade to carry* **150** *passengers).* RUNS DAILY (Sundays included). Saloon to accommodate **80** passengers

ELECTRIC LIGHT. THE DECKS ARE SHADED BY LARGE AWNINGS.

Brighton & Rottingdean Electric Sea Railway

SERVICE FOR WEEK ENDING **OCT. 1st, 1899** (Weather and circumstances permitting).

HIGH-WATER AT BRIGHTON.		
Sep.		a.m.	p.m.
25	M	2 39	3 0
26	T	3 23	3 49
27	W	4 18	4 49
28	T	5 26	6 7
29	F	6 54	7 37
30	S	8 14	8 47
31	S	9 17	9 40

It is preferable for passengers to leave the Aquarium Station somewhat earlier than the times stated below.

VOLK'S ELECTRIC RAILWAY CARS RUN EVERY SIX MINUTES.

BRIGHTON TO ROTTINGDEAN & VICE VERSA.

From BRIGHTON—			Not on Sunday.		Not on Sunday. * *	*From* ROTTINGDEAN—			Not on Sunday.		Not o Sunda * *
		a.m.	p.m.	p.m.	p.m.				††	p.m.	p.m.	p.m.
†AQUARIUM, V.E.R.	dep..	10 55	12 10	2 55	4 35	ROTTINGDEAN	dep..	11 40	12 50	3 50	5 45
KEMP TOWN	,, ..	11 0	12 20	3 0	4 40	*OVINGDEAN	,, ..	11 45	12 55	3 55	5 50
*OVINGDEAN	arr..	11 30	12 40	3 40	5 20	KEMP TOWN	arr..	12 20	1 25	4 40	6 25
ROTTINGDEAN	,, ..	11 35	12 45	3 45	5 25	†AQUARIUM	,, ..	12 30	1 35	4 50	6 35

Short Trips of half-an-hour are made from Brighton at times shown below.
10.15, 2.15, ALSO AT 12.50 ON SUNDAY ONLY.

Fare 6d. CHILDREN UNDER 12 HALF-PRICE.

✳OVINGDEAN.—The Car will call at Ovingdean Jetty to set down or take up Passengers when required.

† The Cars on Volk's Electric Railway do not run on Sundays.

†† Leave Rottingdean at 12.5 and 4.0 on Sunday.

* * If the weather be unfavourable these Trips will not be made.

FARES BETWEEN **BRIGHTON** (KEMP TOWN) **& OVINGDEAN** OR **ROTTINGDEAN**, Single, **6**d. Return, **1**,

Children under 12 Half Fares. *BICYCLES (if room be available) and DOGS (single journey)* **6d.**

The ROTTINGDEAN COMPANY'S TICKETS can be obtained (Sundays excepted), at the Aquarium Station Volk's Electric Railway in which case the fares for Volk's Electric Railway are:—

Single, 1d.; Return, 2d.

PICTORIAL DESCRIPTIVE SOUVENIR, Sold on Car and at Stations, 2d.

IMPORTANT NOTICE. N.B.—Although every endeavour will be made to ensure punctuality and regular running the Company will not hold itself liable in any way for loss or inconvenience to passengers owing to any delays or interruptions to the service from any cause whatever, and **Passengers** are booked and conveyed solely on these conditions. The chief object of the Company is to provide a Sea airing in the safest and most pleasant manner possible. **P.T.O**

A timetable which survives for the week ending 1 October 1899 shows that there was a daily service of four return trips to Rottingdean (except on Sundays when there was two) taking around 1 hour 45 minutes to complete. In addition, there were two short 30-minute trips out from Banjo Groyne (three on Sundays). The fares were 6d single and 1s return to Rottingdean and 6d return for the short trips. Children under twelve travelled at half-price. Bicycles (if room was available) and dogs (single journey) were an additional 6d. The car would call at Ovingdean Gap Jetty to set down or take up passengers as required, but if the weather was unfavourable the last return journey of the day (leaving Banjo Groyne at 4.40) would not be made. It was stated that the connecting Volk's Electric Railway did not operate on Sundays, and the company was not liable in any way for the loss or inconvenience to passengers because of delays and interruptions to the service. A pictorial descriptive souvenir of the Daddy-Long-Legs was available to purchase on the car and at stations for 2d.

The service remained similar in 1900 although short trips in and out from Banjo Groyne increasingly became the norm, enabling more people to experience a ride through the sea, albeit a shorter one. Yet the company's finances failed to improve, which was not helped when the service had to be suspended during July and August 1900 after the track was damaged by the scour from the construction of two concrete groynes to help prevent erosion of the cliffs. There were also complaints that the track was generally unsafe. Then, on 1 September 1900, Brighton Corporation gave Magnus Volk two months' notice to relocate the track at Kemp Town 200 feet southwards to make room for groyne extensions. The service was officially suspended in February 1901 after the Borough Surveyor removed a section of track between the Banjo and Black Rock groynes.

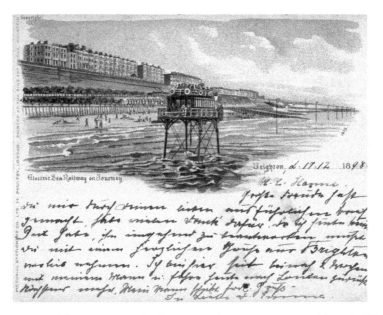

This pretty court card has a message in German and was sent to an address in Hannover on 17 December 1898. The publisher of the card was the Pictorial Stationery Company, London, and it was printed at the Fine Arts Works in Holstein.

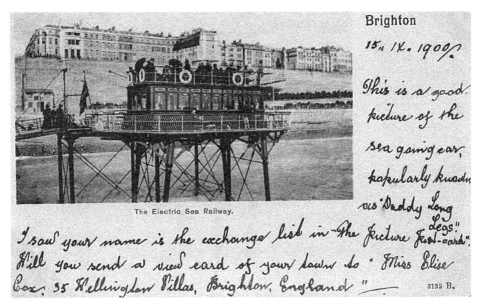

The Electric Sea Railway.

The publisher of this postcard is unknown, and it was posted to Naples on 15 September 1900 with the sender remarking: 'This is a good picture of the sea going car, popularly known as "Daddy long legs".'

Railway-on-Sea, Brighton.

The sender of this postcard has written: 'This is the railway that runs through the sea to a place near. We had a big storm yesterday and the line got damaged. I want to go on it when it is alright again, it must be so funny to go through the sea in a train'. Sadly for them, by the time the card was sent on 13 November 1901 the service had been suspended.

Sea-going Car

474

The Daddy-Long-Legs continued to remain a popular postcard subject after closure, as evident from this postcard, which was produced by Galic, Paige & Co. of Western Road, Hove, in about 1903. This shows the car without any lifebuoys.

SEA CAR, BRIGHTON

St. John's, Withdeane, Near Brighton.

Sep. 1st '03.

Dear Mr. Pettie.

Many thanks for your card which arrived safely. I am glad to see y⁻ memory is in such good order – shewing that y⁻ method is good. I shall be glad to have the letter you speak of. It is good of you to have written for me. – Hope you will enjoy the Hague. When are you coming to England to carry out our little plan? – I am having a glorious time. Kind regards to both yr sons. E.V.

A hand-finished postcard of the sea-going car sent to Leipzig on 1 September 1903. The safety railing of the car has been clumsily redrawn and the flag on the jetty, which should read 'Brighton and Rottingdean', has been redrawn as a Union flag!

This postcard was printed in Saxony, Germany, and was posted to Trouville in France on 18 August 1899. It shows a well-loaded *Pioneer* ready to depart, viewed by spectators on the beach.

Posted to Sydenham on 14 September 1902, this postcard shows that, in fine weather at least, the upper deck of the saloon was the most popular place to sit on the car.

Issued by the Wrench Series, this postcard was sent to Greenock on 12 January 1904 with the curious message: 'This is a sample of the Belfast new cars going to run to Bangor.' Was the message a joke, or was there a plan to run a sea-going car in the north of Ireland?

A popular postcard image of the Daddy-Long-Legs was this view by Stengel & Co. of Dresden, which is available in at least three variations. This card was posted to Edinburgh on 23 January 1904.

This card by Raphael Tuck & Sons, featuring the Brighton crest, was sent as 'one for your collection' on 7 February 1905.

Featuring the same image as the previous postcard, the publisher has added people to the beach and airbrushed out the trolley arms of the car.

Arthur Corder of Brighton issued a series of postcards of the Daddy-Long-Legs, all confusingly captioned that it was destroyed by a gale in December 1896, but showing photographs of the rebuilt railway after that date!

This Corder card shows a queue of passengers awaiting the arrival of *Pioneer* in company with a crowd of curious onlookers on the Banjo Groyne. Two confectionery sellers wait to cash in on the crowds.

The Daddy-Long-Legs was also featured in the view albums of Brighton issued at the time. These four lithographs of the railway were featured in the *Camera Series of Views of Brighton.*

THE SEA RAILWAY, BRIGHTON.

Pioneer approaching the Banjo Groyne Jetty pictured in *32 Photographic Views of Brighton and Neighbourhood*, published by Calcutt & Bevis. In between *Pioneer* and the jetty, Lewes Crescent be seen up on the cliff top.

Volk initially thought that the Daddy-Long-Legs was worth saving and planned a new Brighton terminus further east at Black Rock on the Brighton–Rottingdean boundary. This would have connected with an extension of Volk's Electric Railway to Black Rock, which had been given planning permission by Brighton Corporation after the abandonment of the Brighton & Rottingdean Seashore Electric Railway between Banjo Groyne and Black Rock. On 21 February 1901, Richard St George Moore submitted plans for a new deviation line, 2 miles, 2 furlongs and 7 chains in length, from Black Rock to Rottingdean on a viaduct. Moore and Volk also presented a plan, on 26 June 1901, for a proposed timber gangway over the southern end of the Black Rock Groyne to form a landing stage if the line was to continue to run through the sea. However, the viaduct line was their preferred choice and this was authorised by an Act of Parliament on 23 June 1902, which also sanctioned the abandonment of the Brighton & Rottingdean Seashore Electric Railway. Yet, Volk soon realised that continual expensive maintenance costs caused by stormy seas would have made the viaduct line unviable and the scheme was quickly abandoned.

[2 EDW. 7.]   *Brighton and Rottingdean Seashore*   [Ch. xiii.]
                Electric Tramroad Act, 1902.

CHAPTER xiii. /3

An Act to authorise the Brighton and Rottingdean   A.D. 1902.
   Seashore Electric Tramroad Company to divert a
   portion of their existing and authorised Tramroad
   in the County of Sussex and to construct a new
   Tramroad in lieu thereof and for other purposes.

[23rd June 1902.]

WHEREAS by the Brighton and Rottingdean Seashore Electric Tramroad Act 1893 (herein-after called "the Act of 1893") the Brighton and Rottingdean Seashore Electric Tramroad Company (herein-after called "the Company") was incorporated and authorised to construct a tramroad along the seashore from Brighton to Rottingdean in the county of Sussex with a jetty or landing-stage at Rottingdean and to raise twenty thousand pounds by shares and five thousand pounds by borrowing:

The Act of Parliament of 23 June 1902 which sanctioned the abandonment of the Brighton & Rottingdean Seashore Electric Tramroad. The proposed new tramroad, to be laid out on a timber viaduct, was never built.

Cruising Under White Cliffs to Closure

Now let's look at the rest of the line travelling eastwards to Rottingdean. Journeying out from Banjo Groyne, the white stucco terraces and crescents of Marine Parade, Kemp Town, could be seen on the cliff top before the cliffs of Black Rock were reached, where three doomed properties (Black Rock House, the Abergavenny Arms and the Cliff Creamery) lay perilously close to the cliff edge. Further east and built safely back from the cliff edge up on the hillside was Roedean, an independent day and boarding school for girls. The school had been relocated to this site from Kemp Town in 1898, into buildings designed by architect Sir John Simpson. 2 miles from Brighton, the intermediate landing stage at Ovingdean Gap was reached. Plans for the 'Greenways Jetty' at the site were received by the Board of Trade from Richard St George Moore on 11 November 1896 and consent to build it was granted on 23 March 1897. The design was almost identical to the pier built at Rottingdean in 1895 and consisted of a sloping landing stage 220 feet in length and 40 feet wide. However, it was to be built of wood rather than light steel as at Rottingdean. An amended plan was submitted by Moore on 19 February 1897 showing a landing platform on the seaward side of the railway, but this was not built.

Passengers can be seen boarding *Pioneer* at Banjo Groyne, ready for a journey through the sea towards Rottingdean. The times of both the Rottingdean and short trips are advertised on the jetty.

jebe von ihnen
trägt bie eine
Seite bes ei=
fernen Gerü=
ftes, auf ber
fich bie für bie
Reifenben be=
ftimmte Platt=
form befinbet.
Von ben vier
Füßen biefer
Eifenkonftruk=
tion ruht jeber
auf einem mit
vier Räbern
verfehenen

Meereifenbahn zwifchen Brighton unb Rottingbean.

Pioneer travelling through the sea in an engraving reproduced in a German newspaper of the time, which shows the international interest in this unique railway. The caption can be translated to 'Sea railway between Brighton and Rottingdean'.

The Regency splendour of Kemp Town overlooked the Brighton section of the sea-going railway and Arundel Terrace was situated at the eastern end of Marine Parade, adjoining Lewes Crescent. Featuring impressive Doric porches, the terrace was built for Thomas Read Kemp by Amon Wilds and Charles Busby in 1824–8. This postcard was published *c.* 1907 in the Brighton Palace Series.

Above left and right: Pioneer is seen heading towards the Brighton terminus in these two photographs taken by Ellis Kelsey in *c.* 1897. Kelsey was an amateur photographer from Eastbourne whose work was exhibited at the Royal Photographic Society in London.

Pioneer is seen travelling through the sea in this view taken from the beach and issued as a postcard *c.* 1910. The caption says: 'The Sea-going car, which formerly ran between the Banjo Groyne and Rottingdean (Destroyed in a gale, December 1896).' The caption gives the impression that the line never ran again, but of course it was reopened in July 1897 and was not officially abandoned until June 1902.

This is another Ellis Kelsey view of the railway and is an unusual image taken from the upper deck of *Pioneer* looking towards the Black Rock Groyne. It shows a good view of one of the cable supporting poles, a line which can be seen curving around the groyne.

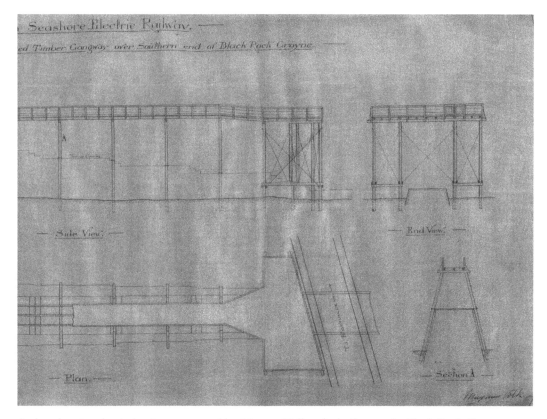

A plan showing the timber jetty proposed by Magnus Volk to be built over the Black Rock Groyne in 1901 if the sea-going car service was restored to Rottingdean from a new terminus at Black Rock. The service was never resumed and so the jetty was not built.

A postcard showing the Black Rock Groyne, which would have become the new Brighton terminus for the Daddy-Long-Legs.

The cliffs at Black Rock are shown on the above postcard published by E. A. Schwerdtfeger & Co. and sent to Birmingham on 11 June 1911. The Daddy-Long-Legs would have run through the sea to the right of the photograph. The properties standing perilously close to the cliff edge are Black Rock House, Abergavenney Arms and the Cliff Creamery café, which were demolished by 1932. In the distance is the famous Roedean school.

This postcard is also by E. A. Schwerdtfeger and shows the doomed properties from the east. Brighton Marina now dominates the area below the cliff. You will meet the gentleman and his dog again twice more in this book!

Located on the cliff top east of Black Rock, we see Roedean Farm very close to the cliff edge in *c.* 1910 after a landslip. Roedean School is on the cliff just behind the farm. The sewage ventilation shaft chimney seen in the background was demolished in 1933.

Another card by E. A. Schwerdtfeger, showing the man and his dog we met at Black Rock sitting upon the cliffs to the east of the remains of the farm, which were removed in the 1930s. The trackbed of the sea-going railway can just be made out on the left of the card.

Roedean School dominated the cliff top between Black Rock and Rottingdean. The school was opened on this site in 1898, during the short life of the Daddy-Long-Legs, having moved from Kemp Town. The buildings, set in 118 acres, were designed by Sir John Simpson.

In this photograph, *Pioneer* is seen travelling towards Rottingdean at low tide, showing us a good view of the track upon which it ran.

The Daddy-Long-Legs is traveling through a high tide in this photograph from *c.* 1900. An awning has been placed over the upper deck to protect passengers from the sun.

Pioneer travelling through a choppy sea at high tide. The upper deck is closed and there are no lifebuoys or lifeboat on show. The presence of a ladder strapped to the side of the car suggests this is a maintenance or inspection trip.

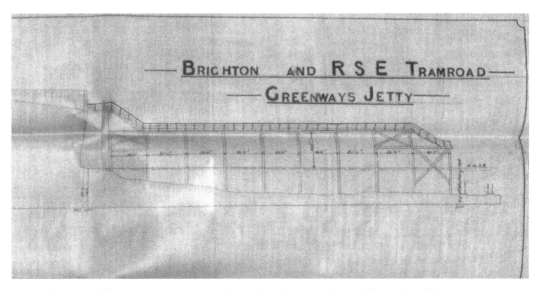

The plan of the Greenways Jetty at Ovingdean Gap as submitted by Richard St George Moore to the Board of Trade in November 1896.

Ovingdean Gap Jetty as built, which was in use from the time the railway reopened in July 1897. This postcard, published by Sidney Hellier, shows the jetty in *c.* 1904 after the closure of the line, with *Pioneer* tied up at the end.

The village of Ovingdean was about a mile away from the jetty along Greenways Road. This postcard shows a general view of the village and was posted on 12 July 1905 with the sender remarking: 'We are staying at this delightful place; the Downs are lovely. Charles the Second before he was king, when he was hiding from Cromwell, was hidden in a secret room in this house, so it makes it very historic.' The house being referred to is Ovingdean Grange, which is on the right of the card.

A rare view taken by a visitor to Brighton in 1904 showing *Pioneer* tied up at the Ovingdean Gap landing stage. Points of interest include a possible nameboard on the jetty and shuttering seen by the track on the south-east corner of *Pioneer*.

The jetty was opened as a request stop when the railway was reopened on 20 July 1897. It appears to have been very lightly used before the service was suspended in February 1901 and officially closed the following year. *Pioneer* was lashed to the end of the Ovingdean jetty after closure and was left to a slow, lingering and rather undignified death. Volk claimed he had no money to maintain the landing stages at Ovingdean Gap and Rottingdean or to pay the outstanding rent of £30 to the Board of Trade, and seemingly washed his hands of his former pride and joy seashore railway. It was left to J. J. Clark of Goldstone Farm, Hove, a former director of the Brighton & Rottingdean Seashore Electric Tramroad Company, to remove in 1906–7 the shore end of the Ovingdean jetty, to deter trespassers, and sections of rail close to the jetty. By February 1910 both *Pioneer* and the jetty had been dismantled for scrap and all that was left were a few pile stumps that could be seen at low tide.

From Ovingdean Gap, it was a further 0.9 miles to the end of the line at Rottingdean Pier. The pier was first proposed in 1892 and Moore's design showed it to be 220 feet in length and 40 feet wide with five sets of supporting columns, two of them at the end of the structure. The original design showed the pier being reached by a stepped-down entrance from the cliff top (as built at Ovingdean Gap), but eventually a wooden right-angled slope from Rottingdean Gap up to the pier was provided. Agreements were reached with the Crown regarding the foreshore and with the Marquis of Abergavenney about the beach and cliff top (the latter leased by Henry Willett), and Board of Trade assent to build the pier was granted on 23 August 1894.

The pier was constructed of light steel by C. G. Reed & Son and stood 30 feet clear of high water with steps leading down from the 60-foot-high pier head to the landing stage. Beneath the pier was the railway's original generator of electricity, which was made redundant when a direct supply was obtained from Brighton Corporation in 1898. The pier was opened on 11 June 1895 for people to walk upon, nearly eighteen months before the line was opened.

Above: The shore end of the disused Ovingdean Gap Jetty was removed during the winter of 1906–7 to deter trespassers.

Below: For such an elegant and unusual railway vehicle, which attracted such interest, it is rather sad to see this view of *Pioneer* tied up forlornly at the end of Ovingdean Gap Jetty.

CLIFFS BETWEEN BRIGHTON AND ROTTINGDEAN.

0137

Above: The sad end for both *Pioneer* and Ovingdean Gap Jetty came during the winter of 1909/10. This postcard by E. A. Schwerdtfeger shows the jetty mainly gone and a barge ready to take away the materials. The deck of *Pioneer* has been cleared away, leaving just the platform and legs.

Below: A postcard from 1933 showing the new undercliff walk at Ovingdean Gap where the jetty once stood. The walk, which was built between Brighton and Rottingdean, was opened on 4 July 1933. In the distance can be seen Roedean School and the soon-to-be demolished sewage ventilation chimney.

OVINGDEAN STEPS, NEW COASTAL PROMENADE, BRIGHTON.

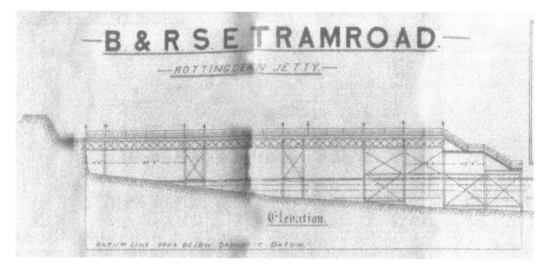

We have now reached Rottingdean and this is Richard St George Moore's original design for the pier (as it was generally known in preference to being termed a jetty), dated 23 August 1894. The pier was largely constructed as shown, except there is no electricity generating plant under the pier and the entrance is shown to be reached from the clifftop. A wooden ramp up from the Gap would eventually be built.

This photograph curiously shows the pier as built but without its generating plant. This perhaps dates it to the period 1895–6, before the line was opened, or just after the pier had been repaired following the storm of December 1896 and the generating plant had yet to be installed. There are also no railings on the landing stage levels.

Photographs of *Pioneer* at Rottingdean Pier appear to be few and far between. This view of the pier is quite an early one: it shows the chimney for the generating plant, which was removed after the electricity supply for the line was obtained from Brighton Corporation in 1898. Passengers can be seen boarding the car for the journey to Brighton.

This view of *Pioneer* at Rottingdean Pier was taken towards the end of the railway's life and shows the canopy on the upper deck of *Pioneer* to shade passengers from the sun seen in the later photographs of the car.

April 3rd 04

Cliffs at Rottingdean.

A postcard used in 1904 showing the shore end of the pier with its ticket hut and entrance gates. The building marked 'restaurant' on the cliff top (this area of the cliff was known as the 'Quarter Deck') would eventually become a victim of coast erosion.

Rottingdean from Beach

A postcard view taken from the end of the pier looking towards the village and Manor Terrace/High Street South. The white building centre left is the White Horse Hotel, which was rebuilt in 1934.

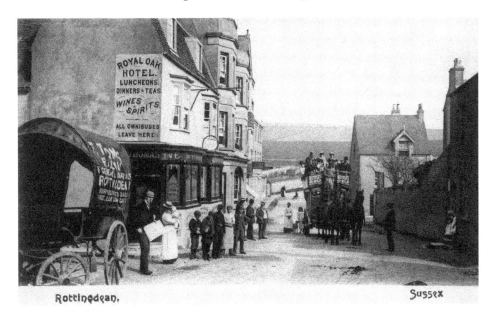

Walking up High Street South from the pier we reach the crossroads with the main coast road through the village (now the A259). This Mezzotint postcard from *c.* 1904 shows the now demolished Royal Oak Hotel, which ran its own horse bus service to Brighton station for a fare of *6d.* The bus is seen loaded up and ready to depart.

This postcard, also by Mezzotint, and posted on 15 June 1907, shows the top end of the High Street looking north towards The Green. The photographer has managed to gather an interesting selection of people for his photograph, including a horse and cart, mother and pram, and two children.

We have reached The Green, where Rottingdean's two most famous, and therefore most photographed, houses were situated. This postcard by village photographer William Bowles in *c.* 1904 features the residence of the Pre-Raphaelite painter Sir Edward Burne-Jones. He passed away in 1898 but the house was still being used at the time by his family. Beacon Mill can be seen up on the hill behind.

Bowles has now turned his attention to The Elms, the home of Rudyard Kipling between 1897 and 1902 before he moved to Batemans to gain some privacy away from the hordes of Brighton tourists who came to view his house. For this delightful postcard the photographer has assembled a group of boys, complete with donkey and makeshift guns, parading outside Kipling's house. I wonder how many of the boys survived the First World War when they had real guns?

Another postcard by William Bowles, who was also a blacksmith (until 1901) and then a church verger and parish clerk, which is another fine study of The Green. Note the early motor car leaving the rear of the large house known as The Dene and horse power of the more traditional kind on the right. The card was sent on 5 April 1907.

Another fine car features in this view of the pond on The Green with Kipling's house in the background. The card was produced by J. Welch & Sons of Portsmouth and was posted on 10 October 1911.

Rottingdean Pier received its first visit from *Pioneer* on the ceremonial opening day of 28 November 1896, but as mentioned earlier, the lack of a second car, bad weather and other operating difficulties meant that by 1900 there were fewer journeys along the line to Rottingdean. Indeed, photographs showing *Pioneer* at Rottingdean Pier are rare. The pier came to assume the role of a traditional seaside pier with its use as a promenade and for fishing. Rudyard Kipling, who lived at The Elms in the village between 1897 and 1902, enjoyed taking his children to the beach and is said to have fished from the pier. Kipling's first cousin was novelist Angela Thirkell, who often visited Rottingdean as a child to visit her grandfather, Pre-Raphaelite painter Edward Burne-Jones. In her book *Three Houses* (1931) she describes seeing the Daddy-Long-Legs arrive at Rottingdean:

By this time a little crowd was collecting on the pier and if my brother and I could find a suitable escort (for we were never allowed to do anything alone, possibly with reason), we had permission to join it. An uncle, or good-natured Julian Ridsdale would volunteer to look after us and off we would go to see the arrival of the Daddy-Long-Legs. This was the most preposterous machine which came on railway lines through the sea from Brighton every day. Huge blocks of concrete had been laid in the sea with lines on them and along these rolled a kind of elevated platform with four immensely long legs ending in great boxes with wheels inside them. It was more like a vision of the Martians than anything you ought to see at a peaceful seaside village. We were never allowed to go on it, partly because no grown-up thought it amusing enough to go with us and partly because it had a habit of sticking somewhere opposite the ventilating shaft of the Brighton main sewer and not being moved until nightfall. When it had discharged its passengers at the pier it took on a fresh load and stalked back to Brighton leaving us in gaping admiration.

Rottingdean   The Pier and cliffs

Moving back to the seafront, we see the pier from the clifftop to the east in one of Hellier's 'Original and Exclusive' postcards, sent on 11 July 1905.

A fine postcard view of the pier showing it open for the public to enjoy. In the background can be seen Ovingdean Gap Jetty and *Pioneer*.

A further view by William Bowles, who lived at Pekin Cottage in the village. This card of the pier from the clifftop was sent from that address by his daughter May. Both bathing machines and tents (operated by 'Trunky' Thomas) can be seen on the beach.

The pier as seen from the eastern side of the beach on a postcard sent by Adela on 21 August 1911 to Miss Lander to inform her Rottingdean was a lovely place and she was enjoying herself very much. Both the beach and pier are almost completely deserted.

During his time at Rottingdean, Rudyard Kipling enjoyed taking his family down to the beach and it is said he partook of a spot of fishing from the pier. Kipling's son John can be seen sitting on the beach with the pier in the background. John was sadly to lose his life during the First World War (as I suppose did most of the little boys seen parading outside Kipling's house) at the Battle of Loos on 27 September 1915.

A postcard of a family on the beach underneath the pier, which clearly shows the two separate sections of the structure: the steel main section and the wooden access ramp. The card was sent on 22 September 1911 with the sender bemoaning: 'This is Jim and I on the beach at Rottingdean and its an awful one of me!'

The pier is seen from the west in this postcard posted on 15 May 1906 to Arthur in Brockley by Lily, who writes: 'How would you like to be sailing a boat on this water and paddling as the little boys are doing here.'

This view of the pier was taken on a day when the beach and pier are deserted: perhaps it was early in the morning? The card was posted to Worthing on 3 December 1907.

An excellent real photographic postcard of the pier, sent on 13 April 1910. The pier head is completely unadorned save for the flagpole.

Although the subject of William Bowles' postcard is the rough sea, he has also given us a rare close-up view of the seaward end of the pier. The card is unfortunately not dated but it must have been taken towards the end of the pier's life. The generating plant building under the pier remained *in situ* despite being disused since 1898.

The pier only saw a few visits from the Daddy-Long-Legs in its last year of operation in 1900. Following the closure of the line, the pier was opened on occasions for the public to enjoy by J. J. Clark, who was prepared to pay the outstanding rent to the Board of Trade and take it over. On 30 October 1908 he informed the BOT that 'this jetty is in good condition and could be used, as it formerly was, as a promenade by the Rottingdean inhabitants and visitors on payment of a small toll. It might be lengthened, under a Provisional Order, so as to admit of its being used as a landing place for pleasure steamers'. The Board of Trade granted powers for the pier to be used as a promenade and for tolls to be levied, but in 1911 Magnus Volk was stirred to report to the BOT that the structure was very dilapidated. On 30 June 1911 the Crown resumed possession of the foreshore where the pier stood, and Volk engaged Messrs Blackmore, Gould & Company (who had offered £40 scrap value) to remove the pier. The work commenced on 11 September 1911 and was completed by early December.

The rails at the Rottingdean end of the line had been removed by Blackmore, Gould & Company in December 1910, but Rottingdean Parish Council remained unhappy that the concrete blocks remained in place on the beach. In 1913 they requested that they should be removed as they were a danger to craft using the new slipway.

This postcard is undated but appears to have been taken *c.* 1910. There is a mast or crane-like contraption on the pier head and both the pier and its ticket office look generally the worse for wear in this view.

The man and dog we saw before at Black Rock and on the cliff near Roedean Farm have now made their way to Rottingdean for another E. A. Schwerdtfeger & Co. view. If you look carefully in the background you can see the barge we saw earlier being used to dismantle Ovingdean Gap Jetty and *Pioneer*. The card was posted on 25 July 1910 and note Cliffe House on the cliff top.

In this view, also by Schwerdtfeger and sent on 30 November 1911, you will see that the seaward end of Cliffe House has tumbled over the cliff. At the time the card was sent, the pier was itself in the process of demolition.

This postcard, posted on 18 July 1911, also shows the truncated Cliffe House. The card, published by the SPP Agency of Richmond Terrace, Brighton, shows the pier being used for storage, including for a boat, just before the demolition of the structure was commenced in September 1911. By December 1911 the pier was no more.

A photograph taken on the pier by William Bowles and sent as a postcard on 11 July 1905. Compare it with the following photograph. The sender, M.S., has put an x above the cottage where they are staying.

This photograph of Rottingdean Gap, taken in July 2018 from where the pier stood, shows that much has changed. The pier itself is long gone and its site is covered by a groyne of large granite stones. The cottage where M.S. stayed is now covered by a large block of apartments called St Margarets.

The Lasting Legacy of Magnus Volk

As recompense for the closure of the Brighton & Rottingdean Seashore Electric Railway between Banjo Groyne and Black Rock, Volk was granted planning permission to extend his Volk's Electric Railway from Paston Place station (now known as Halfway) to Black Rock, which opened in September 1901. The line was extended by knocking out the back of the train shed and crossing Banjo Groyne on the level before veering back across the beach towards Madeira Road on a timber viaduct. The line was powered by the town's 460 V DC mains supply. Sunday running was allowed from 1903, and in 1911 a new bungalow station building was provided at Black Rock. The 1930s saw Volk's Electric Railway truncated at both ends. In 1930 it was shortened by 200 yards at the western end when a new Aquarium station was opened on 27 June 1930 and 1937

Following the suspension of the sea-going car service in February 1901 (and abandonment of the Banjo Groyne–Black Rock section), Volk was granted permission to extend his Volk's Electric Railway from Paston Place to Black Rock, which was opened in September 1901. The landing stage on the Banjo Groyne for the Daddy-Long-Legs was quickly dismantled and the groyne was crossed on the level by the new extension to Volk's Railway, as seen on this postcard.

Another view of Volk's Electric Railway at Banjo Groyne. This postcard was produced by the prolific Brighton postcard publisher A. W. Wardell in *c.* 1910.

After crossing the Banjo Groyne, the Volk's Electric Railway extension ran on a short section of viaduct over the sea before running parallel to Madeira Road. This became a much-photographed section of the line, particularly when the sea was rough, but the height of the beach has since risen to that of the railway and it no longer runs over the sea.

DUKE'S MOUND, KEMPTOWN, BRIGHTON.

This postcard, published by E. A. Schwerdtfeger & Co. of London and printed at their works in Berlin *c.* 1910, features Magnus Volk's workshop and office on the left at the foot of Duke's Mound.

TERMINUS OF VOLKS ELECTRIC RAILWAY AT BLACK ROCK BRIGHTON

A postcard view of the new terminus of Volk's Electric Railway at Black Rock, opened in September 1901. The card was published by the Pictorial Centre, 7 Grand Junction Road, Brighton, and shows the line a few years after opening.

Above: A Brighton View Company postcard dating from *c.* 1910. It is worth noting the lady with the barrow of birds and union flags. Plans in 1901–2 to build a new western terminus for the Daddy-Long-Legs at Black Rock Groyne never came to fruition.

Left: A photograph of Magnus Volk in later life, shortly before his death on 20 May 1937. His last public appearance was the opening of a new station at Black Rock, sited 200 yards to the west.

Magnus Volk was laid to rest in St Wulfran's Church, Ovingdean, where he was later joined by his only daughter, Muriel.

We now look at Volk's Electric Railway as it is today. Semi-open car No. 4, dating from 1892, is seen at Aquarium station in July 2018. Also on view is the new station and visitor centre, opened in October 2017.

Another photograph from July 2018, showing car No. 9 at the Halfway (formerly Paston Place) station of Volk's Electric Railway.

A new workshop at Halfway station was also part of the refurbishments to Volk's Electric Railway following the granting of a Heritage Lottery Grant of £1.65 million and it can be seen here in July 2018. Note the level of the beach now at Banjo Groyne compared to when the Daddy-Long-Legs was running!

Volk's Electric Railway car No. 9 at Black Rock station in July 2018. Due to the construction of a deep level drainage tunnel, the station was to be re-sited again in the 1990s at a neo-classical pumping station, which has a small ticket office and toilets.

saw it curtailed at the eastern end by 200 yards to make way for a new bathing pool. The new Black Rock station was officially opened on 7 May 1937 and this saw the last public appearance of Magnus Volk, who died thirteen days later. He was laid to rest in the churchyard of St Wulfran's Church, Ovingdean. His lasting legacy, Volk's Electric Railway, was purchased by Brighton Corporation on 1 April 1939 and after being leased back to the Volk's company for a year was operated by the corporation from 1 April 1940. They continue to run the railway to the present time and between 2015 and 2017 the line was extensively refurbished after a Heritage Lottery grant of £1.65 million was obtained. The improvements included a new Aquarium station with a visitor centre and new workshop at Halfway station. The railway was reopened in October 2017 and normally operates from Easter until then end of October.

And what remains of Magnus Volk's most memorable creation, the Brighton & Rottingdean Seashore Electric Railway? Despite being closed well over a century ago, this most eccentric of railways continues to fascinate all those who read about it and see the old photographs. At low tide, a line of the concrete blocks that supported the rails can still be seen between Brighton Marina and Rottingdean, giving a visible reminder of the line's existence. Stumps of the wooden poles that supported the overhead wire also survive. Models of *Pioneer* grace museums in Brighton and Rottingdean and Magnus Volk's original template model of the sea-going car is on view at the Aquarium station visitor centre, which also displays photographs of the Daddy-Long-Legs and a souvenir trinket box with a picture of it. In recent years a short snippet of film of *Pioneer* travelling through the sea shot by George Albert Smith in 1897 has come to light and can be viewed on the internet. Long gone but clearly not forgotten, the Daddy-Long-Legs remains truly part of Brighton folklore.

And what can we still see to remind us of the Daddy-Long-Legs railway? Well, in addition to the postcards seen earlier in this book, other souvenirs can be found. There is commemorative china, for example, such as this cup belonging to the author.

A souvenir trinket box of the Daddy-Long-Legs on display in the Volk's Railway visitor centre. Guidebooks and view albums also featured the sea-going car, even after it had closed.

Above: Postcards remain the principal collecting source for images of the Daddy-Long-Legs Railway and it can be seen here on this Souvenir of Brighton card issued by Henry J. Smith of 80 Kings Road.

Right: A cabinet card issued by E. Pannell of Brighton in *c*. 1897 showing two views of the Brighton and Rottingdean Electric Sea-going Car.

Brighton & Rottingdean Electric Sea-Going Car.

Magnus Volk's original template model of *Pioneer* (on the right) is seen here on display with another *Pioneer* model at Brighton Museum and Art Gallery. Volk's model is now on display at the Volk's Railway Visitor Centre. Other *Pioneer* models can be found at The Grange in Rottingdean and at Brighton Toy Museum.

The line of concrete blocks between Brighton and Rottingdean that once supported the track are a visible legacy of the railway and can still be seen at low tide. Stumps of the wooden poles which supported the overhead power cable can also be found, as can a few remains of the jetty at Ovingdean Gap.

The Sea Car's One and Only Cousin: Le Pont Roulant

The Daddy-Long-Legs had a French cousin which, as mentioned earlier, may have inspired Magnus Volk to build his seaborne creation. This was Le Pont Roulant (rolling bridge or crane), which transported up to fifty people across the mouth of the River Rance between the twin towns of St Malo and St Servan. At low tide, a causeway was available, but Le Pont Roulant saved a long detour by land at high tide.

Designed by architect Alexandre Leroyer and opened on 26 October 1873, Le Pont Roulant consisted of a 23 x 19.5-foot platform mounted on four sliding legs 20 feet high. At the bottom of the legs were grooved wheels running on rails, 15 feet apart, which at high tide were covered by a considerable depth of water. 'Le Spider' (as it was nicknamed by locals) was propelled by means of a chain worked by a 10 hp steam engine placed in a wooden building at St Servan, but in 1909 it was electrified by its owner, Mr Durand, after the machinery was damaged by fire. The journey took 2 minutes and in 1900 cost 5 centimes.

In 1889 Le Pont Roulant had been damaged by the ship *Vaquelin* and was struck again during the stormy night of 8 November 1922 when the Norwegian vessel *Brawn* broke its moorings and crashed into it. This brought about the end of the rolling bridge and it was officially closed on 20 February 1923 and removed.

This postcard shows Le Pont Roulant travelling across the harbour at St Malo at high tide. The card was posted in 1906 and the sender has written in English: 'This bridge is worked on railway tracks.'

A postcard view looking across from St Servan towards St Malo showing Le Pont Roulant travelling across the harbour at low tide. On the right is the causeway that could be used when the tide was out. The card was published *c.* 1905 by ND, a major French postcard publisher.

Le Pont Roulant at low tide *c.* 1905 by L. L., another big producer of postcards in France. The car seems devoid of any passengers and people are taking advantage of the low tide to walk across the causeway.

The Sea Car's One and Only Cousin: Le Pont Roulant

Côte d'Emeraude

8512. SAINT-MALO — Le Pont Roulant à mer basse - G. F.

Right: The photographer stood on the floor of the harbour to take this postcard of Le Pont Roulant being reflected in the water at low tide *c*. 1903. The wheels of the car were not covered in as was the case with the Brighton Daddy-Long-Legs.

Below: Look at the two men climbing on the tie rods of the legs while Le Pont Roulant is in motion on this postcard – no health and safety or risk assessments then! The card was posted on 21 March 1901.

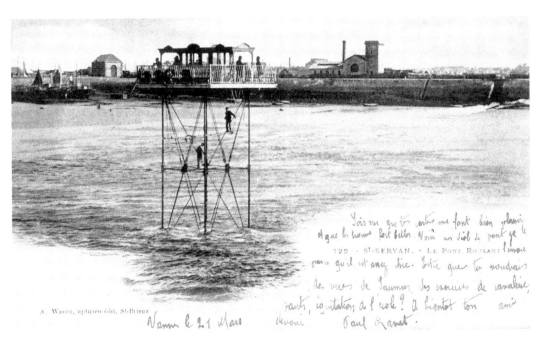

A Waron, opticien-édit, St-Brieuc

722 - St-SERVAN. - LE PONT ROULANT

61   SAINT-MALO. -- Saint-Servan et le Pont Roulant. — LL.

This coloured postcard of Le Pont Roulant at high tide is another by L. L., who also produced cards of towns in Southern England.

1. SAINT-MALO
Le Pont Roulant à marée haute. G. F.

Another colour postcard of Le Pont Roulant, this one locally published in St Malo by Germain *c*. 1910. The card also shows the ferry that operated across the harbour.

SAINT-MALO.
Arrivée du Pont Roulant. — LL.

Le Pont Roulant has docked at St Servan in the lower card by L. L., which was sent in 1910. The ticket office and landing stage at St Malo can be seen on the other side of the harbour.

Acknowledgments

The author wishes to thank Linda Sage for her assistance as always and the help of staff at libraries and archive centres during my research. In addition, I sincerely thank Robert Jeeves, Christopher Horlock and Sam Flowers for their kind permission to use their photographs. The postcards in this book are from the author's own collection, gathered over thirty years of interest in piers and the Daddy-Long-Legs. Many original documents, as well as written and online sources, have been consulted and researched. The written sources include *Three Houses* by Angela Thirkell (1931), *Magnus Volk of Brighton* by Conrad Volk (Phillimore 1971), *Volk's Railways Brighton: An Illustrated History* by Alan A. Jackson (Plateway Press 1993), *Piers of Sussex* by Martin Easdown (The History Press 2009), *East Brighton and Ovingdean Through Time* by Douglas d'Enno (Amberley Publishing 2010) and *Volk's Electric Railway: A Visitor's Guide* (Shrewdale Publishing 2018). Online sources include www.volkselectricrailway.co.uk and www.sussexpostcards.info.

Pioneer photographed by Ellis Kelsey in *c.* 1897 at Rottingdean.

Wave goodbye girls to the car in the sea
As it travels serenely into history
Leaving behind brief memories
And just a touch of jealously
That I never had the chance to see it